MAKE A MASK

Joan Peters and Anna Sutcliffe

MAKE A MASK

B. T. Batsford Limited
London and Sydney

© Peters and Sutcliffe 1975
First published 1975

All rights reserved. No part of this
publication may be reproduced in
any form or by any means without
permission

ISBN 0 7134 3048 6

Filmset by Servis Filmsetting
Ltd, Manchester

Printed in Great Britain by
The Pitman Press, Bath
for the publishers
B. T. Batsford Ltd
4 Fitzhardinge Street,
London W1H 0AH
and 23 Cross Street, Brookvale
NSW 2100, Australia

CONTENTS

ACKNOWLEDGMENT

The authors would like to thank the following for their help and encouragement: Mr R. S. Johnson, Director of Education, Leeds; Miss J. Harland Principal of the James Graham College, Leeds; Mrs M. Norton, Headmistress of West Park High School, Leeds; the staff and students of the James Graham College, especially the students in the main and subsidiary Art and Main English Courses, and the pupils of West Park High School. Also Audrey Mason and Tom Guy for their practical help at very short notice.

Acknowledgment and thanks are also due to Edward Grinham for taking the majority of photographs, and to Freda Copley for figures 115 and 189, Keith Tones for figures 83, 85–9 and 100, Jerry Bird for figures 106, 131, 154 and 157, Harold Mason for figures 168, 169 and 170 and Glyn Jones for figure 188 and two of the colour plates, *The Hag* and the large mask from cardboard.

INTRODUCTION

1 The face is anointed with a generous layer of cream or baby lotion, and gently powdered with metallic gold or silver powder, taking great care to avoid the eyes and mouth. The Egyptian wig and collar are basically felt scraps with beads, string and small metal objects

The making and wearing of masks can help adults and children alike to adopt a new identity. 'Persona' means mask. The need to enhance, disguise or extend oneself is fundamental, and is to be seen in the wearing of all kinds of make-up, jewels and costume.

It is often interesting to see how, when making a mask, a child or student will produce something not unlike himself, but subtly different. Perhaps the usual face in repose – but gold, or a very splendid scarlet affair – quite unlike the person except that it has the sort of opulence that the maker possesses.

Sometimes masks are work for us rather than by us. The immaculate face of a fashion model is an obvious example – the creation of an ideal face, which varies from generation to generation.

Teachers often remark that masks increase children's confidence, enabling them to speak more fluently and expressively or to become more imaginative, creating character in drama work more easily. Even a puppet or a mask on a stick, held up by a child who is unconcealed, will help him to project character and emotion.

Masks that do conceal may be the most ready encouragement to some children and adults to participate in dance drama or theatre.

For those making the masks – whether or not the artists are also the wearers, creative opportunities arise in the transformation of common materials and the engaging in what Tolkien calls 'secondary creation' – the absolute freedom to invent new 'impossible' characters and presences without any need to be 'good at modelling' or 'good at portraits'.

Creating 'presences' whether graphic or sculptural in the form of dolls, puppets, masks or moving bodies in plays, dance or 'events', is one of the most powerful and satisfying art forms.

Masks have power. Young children who are usually happy and rational, can be frightened by them, even when they know who is wearing them, even adults can become uneasy particularly when left alone with one, or with a collection. In controlled conditions this power can extend the imagination.

If masks are used as an opportunity for sheer creativity in the art room or classroom, then these may suggest all kinds of activities: event, productions, storytellings and displays.

We deplore the idea that the 'visual' must always follow, sometimes it can lead:

'Let us use our masks now that we have made them . . . . .'

'If we made some more masks like this we could . . . . .'

'I wonder if we could dance in these the next time . . . . .'

All these suggestions are valid, so also are:

'Can you make forty masks for 'Noyes Fludde' please' (preferably six months in advance).

'If we need masks in the play, will you make them for us?'

'I was thinking of having the fairies masked . . . . .' and so on.

There is no need to prefer one or the other approach, so many ways are good. The production of 'The Tempest' in full pomp, does not rule out the *ad hoc* (and perhaps equally splendid) dance drama that began with that very special mask. Neither need replace the drama event that arose out of idea in normal drama work, and has grown out of improvisation.

Modern ideas about religious education may suggest another use for masks. Children may learn about the history of religious ideas by making and wearing, for example, African ceremonial masks, Inca style death masks or horned animal heads. This would be an exercise in imagination as we do not suggest that complete understanding is possible.

In addition, events of a ceremonious nature, involving quite static poses, may be impressive if a mask is set on a long staff. The next step can be the manipulation of lay figures or large puppets. There are many kinds of expressive drama and many purposes, from satire and melodrama to the most serious ceremony. A series of human figures may be combined in one event. The 'Gods' may be sculptures or even silhouettes, the 'Demons' masked dancers, and the penitent peasants as natural as one wishes.

No doubt, readers will be able to think of many applications of the art of mask making, from helping withdrawn children to express themselves more freely, to their use as part of the most complex work of art.

2　A very fierce lion, made from a simple
card shape with features modelled with
Mod-Roc, the mane from old rope

3　Masks made on wire frames layered
with papier maché, and painted and
decorated. The beards are made from
fringing. Worn simply with plain leotard
and tights for movement and dance

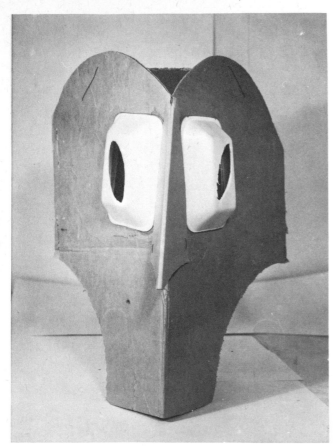

4 and 5 Large simple card mask showing back and front; eyes made from polystyrene containers, the nose is a simple card shape stapled to the base. This simple folded method with cut-away sides, provided a good deep profile

6 and 7 The authors wearing masks which form complete costumes. In 7 note the skilful use of chocolate pack for teeth, the decorative effect of string vest and extension to fingers by means of rolled paper tubes. This method of continuing a mask into a costume is simple, effective and capable of great development; the principle used is a simple 'poncho' ie a large fabric shape (a sheet is ideal) with a hole for the head. In 6, the mask (with rag and wool hair and beard forming an integral part of the costume) is pinched and dyed foam rubber effectively suggesting an unpleasant fungoid creature from science fiction

8 *Bottom* from *A Midsummer Night's Dream*; a wire construction covered with grey fur fabric

9 African style mask; card shape with
paper clumps glued onto face to make
features; painted black and gold, with
nylon and felt hair

10 Mask from Africa in carved wood

MATERIALS

As for many activities in art education, the rule is *keep everything*. Some useful items for collection:

Beads, buttons, haberdashery, feathers, braids, 'baubles', pasta, seeds, dried plants, industrial waste (metal turnings, off cuts etc), beachcombings, scrap, small metal objects of all kinds, any old fabric (curtains, bedding, garments etc), knitted objects (very useful for armour effects), tights and stockings, all papers and cards, plastic and polythene, foil, bright wrappers, in fact anything.

Some suggested new materials and basic equipment.

Scissors, stapler, pins.

Glue eg Marvin-medium (which also serves as a binder or varnish), Polycell or any other cellular paste, Evo-Stick or any other impact adhesive.

Chicken wire and soft wire.

Mod-Roc or any other plaster impregnated fabric.

Plaster, needles and thread, coloured (Ostwald) and black and white papers.

Paints in bright colours. Cellophanes and acetates. Bronze powders (gold, silver and bronze), metallic sprays, twines and string, felt, cheap off-cut fabrics, remnants etc.

11 Keep everything

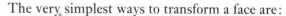

The very simplest ways to transform a face are:
  A grimace
  Hands over eyes, fingers parted
  Long hair
Or by utilising simple objects:
  Glaring down cardboard tubes
  Wearing spectacles
  Improvised glasses (scissors, spanners, etc)
  Stockings or tights
  Children often have to be prevented from painting each others faces in art lessons, but this useful impulse can be turned to creative good. Most of us can remember raiding make-up supplies, and guiltily using mothers or sisters lipstick for scarlet noses or war paint, or perhaps only for a pathetic attempt at a grown-up face.
  Some of the more bizarre make up of recent years – painted 'dolls' eyelashes, red 'dolls' cheeks, blue-lips, deathly white faces etc, are a practice very little changed from childhood. Failing all else, children use mud, exactly as primitive people have done.
  In our experience, children readily learn the possibilities of stage make-up and will help very efficiently during productions, often adding useful

12   A very big dog and a very small kitten

13   I can see you and you can't see me

inventions of their own. Inexperienced adults if given scope, also soon become proficient and inventive for themselves or for children. Of course, we would not undervalue serious make-up classes, courses and demonstrations, as people equipped by such training are worth their weight in gold!

15 I see no ships

16 They're off!

17   Jenny invented and made this mask during the photography session; two small tubes and two buttons

18   All teachers wear glasses

19   . . . and actresses and spies wear dark glasses

20   The fly; sweet round biscuits make compound eyes

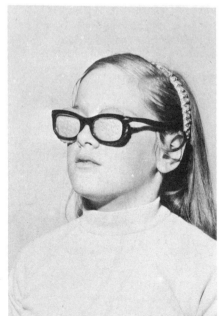

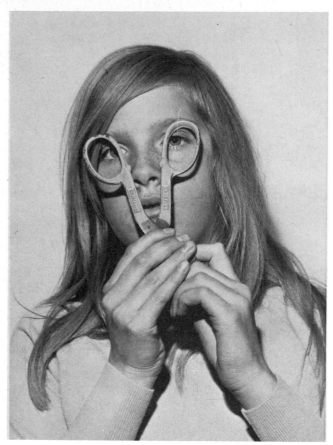

21 Now let me take a closer look

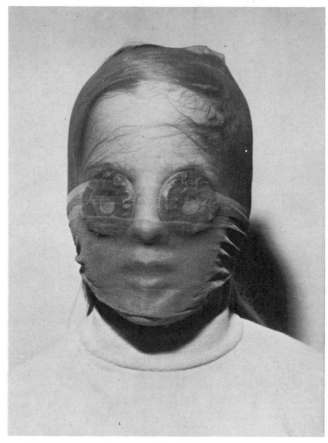

22 Great mystery character with glaring
eyes. A simple nylon stockings with
chocolate biscuits – the possibilities are
many

23   Jenny with a lipstick

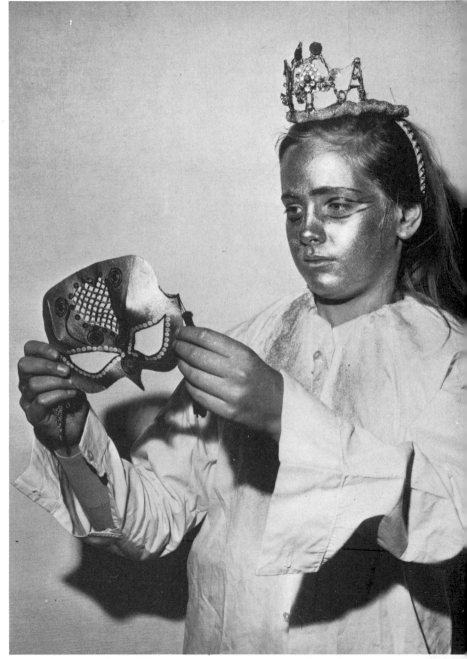

24   Christine preparing to be the Fairy
Queen; her face is silver, the crown is
wire, gold card and beads. The mask is a
painted paper shape

FOUND OBJECTS

Beachcombing, nature walks, scrapyard prowling and other forms of serendipity may yield anything from splendid improvisation and creative thinking, to fine works of sculpture, and provide a basis – as all the methods may – for films, video tapes and creative photography, as well as initiating movement and drama projects.

25 Useful items

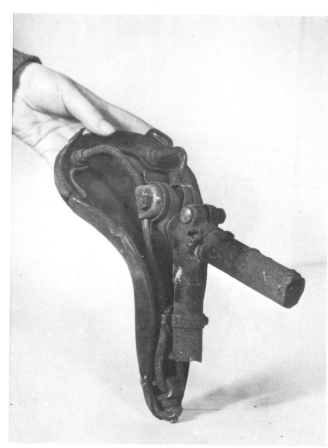

26 Bicycle saddle. Keen mask makers should be in the habit of collecting all kinds of objects which like this one, have a distinct personality

27 Gaskets have many uses, this is one of the simplest

28 We found it, what is it?

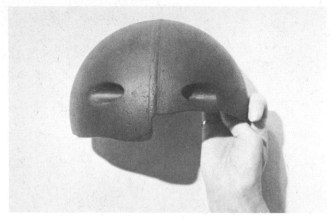

29 and 30   Parts of fishermans floats in
fibreglass, eroded by the tides; 29 is
painted matt black, 30 is just as we found
it. Children soon become adept at seeing
the possibilities of beachcombing

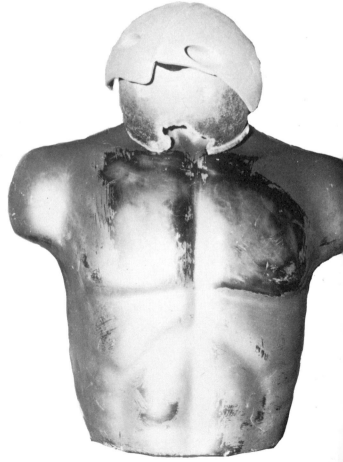

31   Float fragment used with the remnants
of an old enamelled pan and a window
torso to produce a grim presence

32   Shoulder blade of a horse. The bones, begged from a butcher, were buried and subsequently boiled and scraped to clean them, the features made from remaining teeth. Some may find this an unpleasant process, but the effective result will perhaps suggest simpler uses of found objects

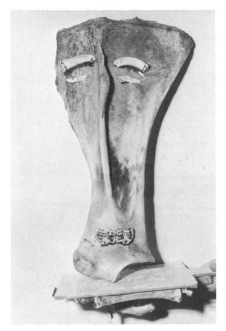

33   Hand mask made from bones glued onto a hardboard shape. This style of mask may be made from chopping boards or table tennis bats

34   Face made from bleached bones found on the beach with 'hair' made from seaweed

35 Wire structure with papier-maché, with eyes from table tennis balls inserted into cardboard cylinders; a further tube forms the nose. Note the ingenious use of found objects for ears and headdress and the plastic packaging material for the teeth

36 *Corn Dolly*. This is the beginning of a large puppet illustrating a myth from New Guinea. The face is the bottom of an old rusty dish mounted on a polystyrene wig stand with the neck removed. The hair is made from wool, shredded hessian, torn net curtains, felt strips etc. All in shades of yellow

37 Top of polythene vat, with handle forming a nose. Wool, felt, buttons and card, plus cut paper shapes, have been used to make this brilliantly coloured, easy to assemble mask; the eyes are table tennis balls

The Hag. This is a huge statue with great presence. A polystyrene wig-stand with neck removed has been used as a foundation for the head, which was inserted into the hood of an old mummy-type sleeping bag. The collar is an old oval bath mat, the hair is seaweed. Plaited wool, bicycle-chains, rusty metal objects, wooden knobs and mussel shells have also been included.

Very large mask based on cardboard carton, otherwise made entirely of newspaper, folded, shredded, cut and torn. Extra height is gained by loosely-rolled newspaper tubes to form the crest.

CARTONS, BAGS AND PACKAGING

One of the most rapid, cheap and not the least effective way of making a mask which may extend well over the body, is by using some of the very wide range of packaging material available. Some packaging presents a pollution problem, but in spite of this it has on occasions been a boon to teachers. If taught not too formally the method encourages creative thinking. Adults should not scorn this method, it has vast possibilities for sculptural effects both comic and serious.

39 A cardboard carton forms the base of
this mask, gaily painted in red and green.
Note the rayon fringe beard

40 A large mask made from an unfolded
cardboard carton, which conveniently
provides shoulders or epaulettes. The hair
is tubular scrim, the features made from
polythene fragments from a packing case,
coloured white, red, gold and black

41 Card mask based on a cardboard
carton, the open ends providing shoulders
or epaulettes. The box is covered with
checked fabric, the eyes are felt, and the
nose is scarlet foam rubber. The hair is
made from black felt strips, and the horns
are pieces of wood. The wearer gets into
the mask through a fabric tube, which is a
useful device

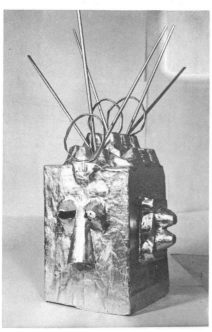

42 Spaceman made from a carton layered with torn newspaper soaked in cellular paste to form the features, plus egg boxes, folded card, rolled newspaper rings and tubes, all painted silver

43 Large carton with small cartons added to form the features. The horns are plastic containers, the tongue is felt. Incisive profile effects can be quickly obtained by a simple arrangement of boxes and cartons

44 Mask made from soggy black paper soaked in cellular paste, piled onto a cardboard box and subsequently dried. This black face is decorated with gold string beads and white polystyrene shapes, a brilliantly painted mouth in scarlet plus black jersey drapes for hair

45   Science fiction character, made from
cartons, paper tubes, light bulbs and other
found objects. Assembled without any
alteration other than gilding

46   Cardboard box plus the lid from an
egg box with holes for eyes, the cheeks
and nose made from clumps of paper,
covered with strips of paper soaked in
cellular paste and painted gold. Hair is
from curled paper strips and horns from
rolled paper tubes

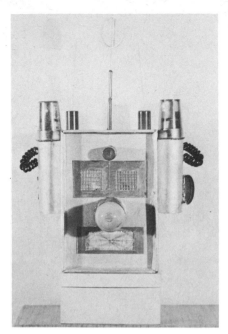
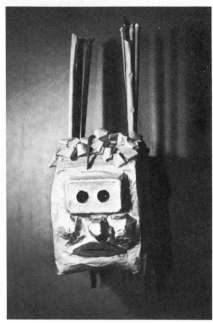

47   Egg boxes may be used too often, but
we like this simple mask made from an
egg box lid, with paper beard and nose
and hessian hair

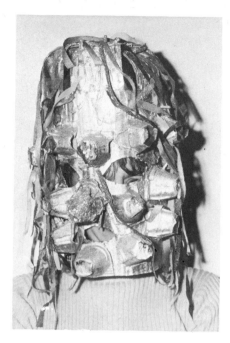

48 Similar to 49, the same components arranged in a different way

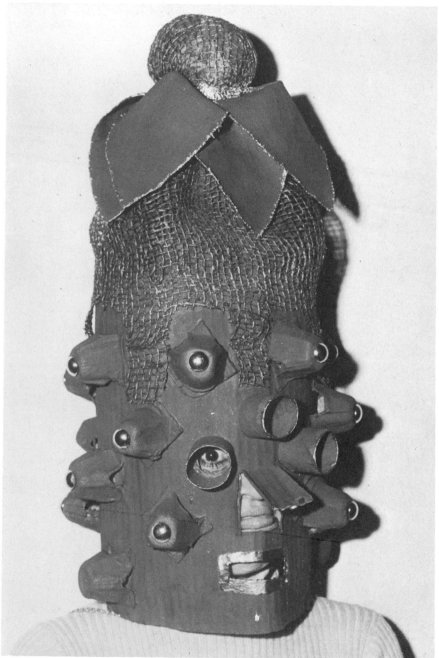

49 Scarlet corrugated card cylinder, scrim turban with paper petals, silver mouth and ubiquitous egg carton

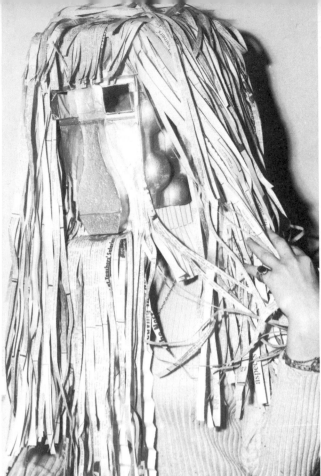

50 to 53   A simple carrier bag, the sides covered with polystyrene apple containers and fringed with corrugated card and newspaper strips. The whole turned upside down and hair and beard fall into place to form a complete mask showing features made from moulded plastic (often found in cosmetic packing)

54 Simple puppet mask. A paper bag with paper features, paper 'feathers' and egg box eyes

55 Very simple paper bags can be richly decorated. These are made from card tubes, curled paper strips and crayon

56 Brown paper bag; note the skilfull use of Easter egg case for nose

57 and 58 Double mask, face back and front; note the good use of printed pattern on the bag. Very quick and easy to make

59 and 60   From owl to pirate in fifteen
minutes

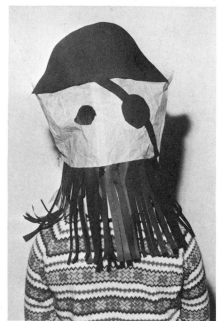

61 and 62   Owl mask based on polystyrene
packing shape. Egg-box eyes, polystyrene
beak, covered with shredded hessian

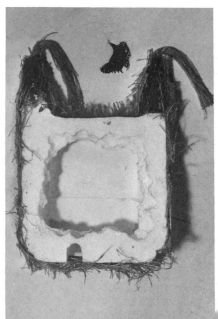

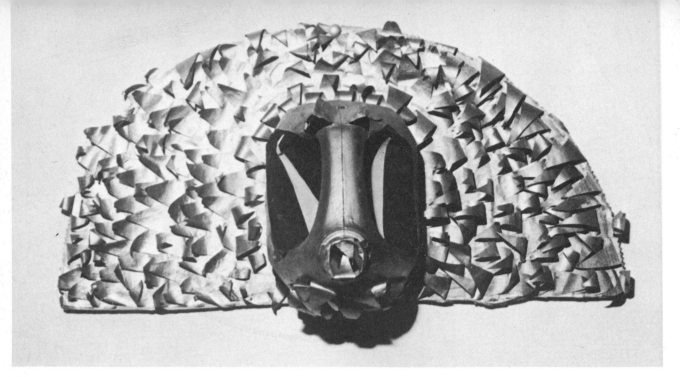

63 and 64 *Sungod*, made from a useful empty Marvin-medium container (any similar plastic container will do just as well). This has been painted gold, and glued to a semi-circle of card trimmed with curled gilded paper, which casts interesting shadows. Either paint the paper gold before cutting and curling, or spray gold when completed

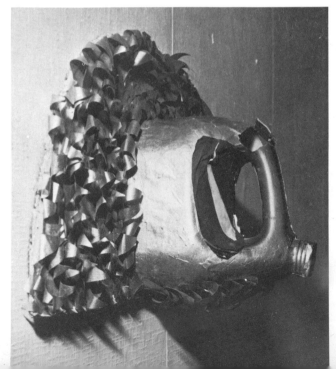

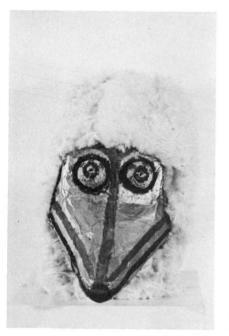

65 and 66 *The Nivram*, the ultimate use
of the gallon Marvin container. The
container is extended with papier maché
and the extension, which forms the face
is painted gold and black, the rest covered
with fur fabric. In addition to being a mask
which covers the head it doubles as a
lap-dog

67 Mask from polythene container. The
features are made from polystyrene
packing, apple box fragments, wool,
metal waste, felt strips and nails. Painted
silver and bright colours

CARD AND PAPER

These materials are very versatile, even very thin paper if bent, shaped, scored, pinned, glued or stapled, may be useful and quite substantial for a time. Size is usually no object, so this range of material is perhaps best for very rapid and often spectacular results.

It may be found useful to try simple rolling, folding, sculpting and shaping experiments first. Paper may be used wet (with Polycell or paste) or dry. Solid papier-mache dries out to be very heavy, a layer of light paper over a loose filling may be preferred. The fillings may be screwed-up paper, paper shavings, computer tape, wood-wool or plastic packing shreds. The results are firm but light in weight.

68 The basic shape of a thin card or cartridge paper mask. This can be cut off or enlarged very easily, the only tools required are scissors and a stapler for the basic shape

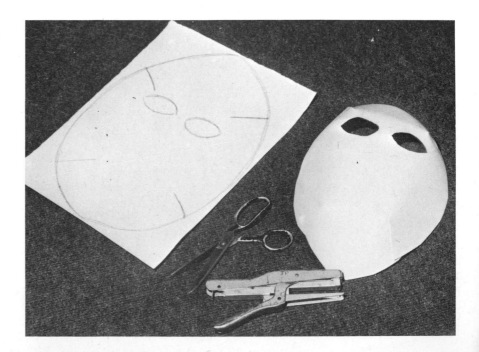

69   Mask in black and yellow cut paper, with rolled paper horns. This mask is flexible but appears rigid when fitted over the head

70   Large flat paper mask inspired by an Aztec death mask, painted and decorated with paper

71   Simple paper shape with curled paper hair and beard; very young children can easily manage to make this kind of mask

72 Mask made entirely of painted sugar paper. This method of shaping flat card or paper is very simple, and capable of deep profile effects

73 Simple mask with features made from cut felt; teeth from white card and eyes from wool. Made very quickly by an eight-year old girl

74 Shredded corrugated packing material forms the hair of the 'beautiful lady' whose paper shaped face is layered with paper and cellular paste. She has an egg box nose, curled paper eyelashes, glittering foil eyes with coloured drawing-pin pupils.

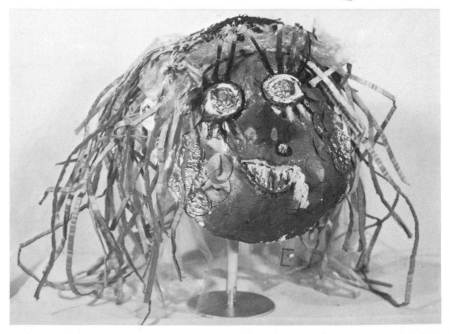

75   A lady not quite so beautiful, made
the same way but with crepe paper hair

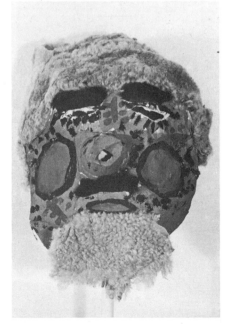

76 and 77   Definitely ugly, using the
same paper shape for face, crepe paper
and lambswool hair

78 to 80 Further variations on the simple paper shaped face, with added curved and folded pieces, and flat or curled paper decoration

81 Effects out of all proportion to the value of the individual masks may be achieved by combining them into gay totem poles and other structures. The pole in this instance is from the middle of a roll of cloth. This provides a good group activity for children of all abilities

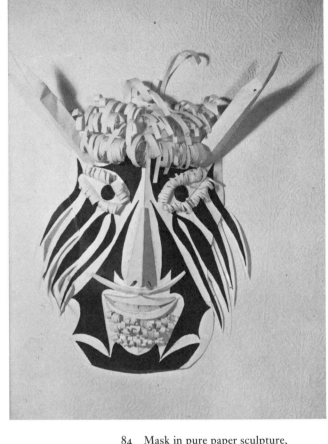

84 Mask in pure paper sculpture, subsequently painted in black and white. Dogged craftsmanship according to the rule book has produced this mask, but the possibilities are endless. The main techniques used are scoring, folding and cutting; it could be the answer to the problem of supplying creative opportunities for children with no great love of handling messy materials

82 Mask by a less able child. Simple card shape painted black and yellow with bead teeth and crepe paper hair

83 Simple flat card shape with features clumped on and held in position with strips of paper soaked in cellular paste; beard of wood-wool, turban of satin, trimmed with braid and painted gold

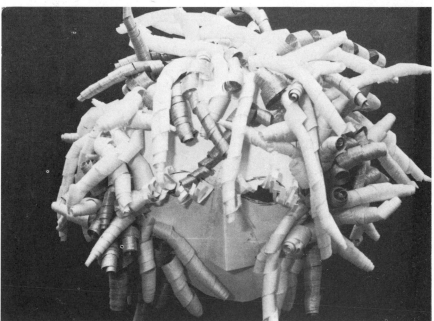

85   Devil mask made by the same
technique as the previous turbanned
mask

86 and 87   Mask simply made by cutting
and scoring card; note the careful use of
wood shavings

90 Simplest possible mask. Made from a card shape, with features built up with crumpled paper; the feathers are held in place by a felt strip

88 Maniac Bird. Note the construction of the beak from cut and folded paper, the head covered in richly coloured fabric 'feathers'. The pieces are fixed together by paper clips, no sticking involved in the actual construction, the fabric however is glued with Marvin-medium. This mask shows how easily a good deep profile can be achieved.

89 Finishing touches being made to the bird with gold braid

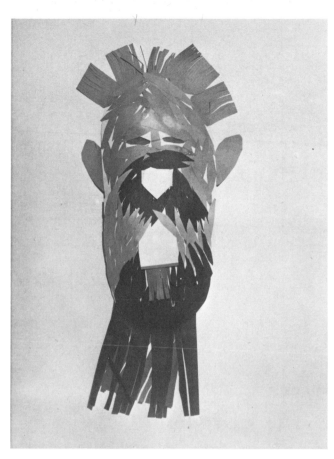

91 to 93 Simple card masks made by
cutting and stapling with plaited or curled
paper hair, features in paint or paper
sculpture

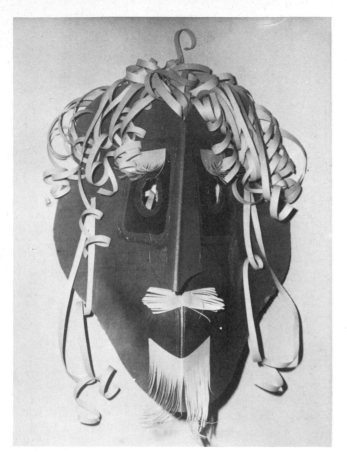 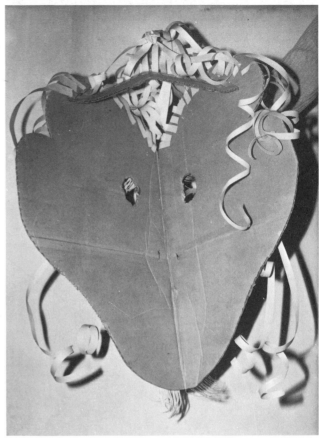

94 and 95   Front and back of simple
mask in stout card clearly showing
construction. Achieved simply by folding
deeply and adding a simple folded nose-
piece. Fringed and looped paper, boldly
painted eyes and a little aerosol paint
spraying complete the effect

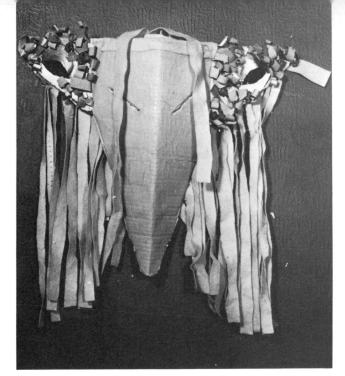

96 A very simple mask from card, painted bright scarlet and with felt strips and paper curls added. Quick and easy to make; suitable for improvised drama work

97 Mask in corrugated card with egg box pieces added. The face is darted to shape, and shells, beads and fabric are added. This mask is very subtle in colour, being dull gold with dark green and pink detail

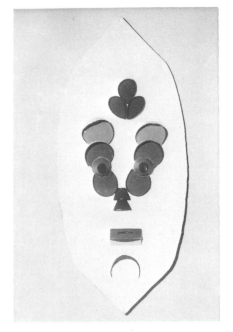

98 Simple shape in card, with cut circles, ovals and stand-away crescents, painted in black, green and white. This mask is very simple, but the shadow pattern can be quite effective

Rolled paper tubes are light and firm, and require very little fixing, extending the head and parts of the body (see the fingers on illustration 7) very effectively for little labour and no expense. We recommend these.

99 Simple card mask with card nose. Carefully painted red and white on black, the crest is made from gold paper tubes. The mask was made on a flat piece of card and while wet with paint was bent round a cylinder, setting into a curve while drying. When painting masks like this, take care to make lines and shapes definite, otherwise a blurred mess may result

100 With rolled paper tubes, polythene carton nose, wood-wool eyebrows and beard; this is a very rapidly made mask

King's mask, in wire structure covered with layers of pasted newspaper painted dark gold, dark red and black paint added. Gold sequin eyelids and hair of black paper curls entirely covering back of head. The beard is of gold-painted newspaper. Crown of rubber-backed carpet and felt. Trimmed with beads and twigs. Not a quickly-made mask but the result is rewarding.

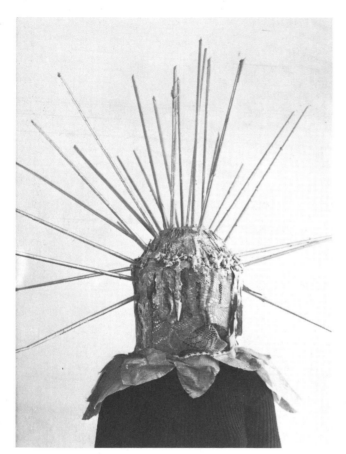

101 Cardboard helmet, entirely covering the head, with eye grills all the way round made from silver-painted cotton curtain net; added paper tubes and decorations of pins, beads and nails dipped in Marvin-medium, sprayed and painted silver

102 Mask with wire frame, covered with layers of newsprint; 'hair' of shredded green cellophane, decorated with rolled paper tubes, the whole painted gold.

OPPOSITE
'Aztec' masks from simple paper shapes covered in two layers of torn paper and Polycell and allowed to dry before a collage of metallic wrapping papers and colours from magazines were applied.

Additional trimmings made from beads, finge, rags and feathers. As a restult of making these in an art lesson and wearing them for fun in the art class, the idea of a dance drama grew, involving the music and

P.E. departments. Further items of costumes were added, ie jewellery and 'aprons' over leotards and tights, and the whole exercise finally involved thirty children

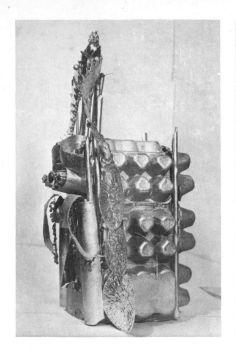

103 and 104   Corrugated card mask, extended by means of card and paper tubes of varying sizes. Additional decoration of stiff gilt paper, beads, Christmas tree baubles and flattened silver foil pie-cases. This is large and impressive

105 Mask with a very strong profile, made from clumps of paper pasted down with glued paper strips onto a simple card shape. Hair and beard from shredded paper, with paper tube crown. This began completely flat, and was drastically bent when wet and pliable. This kind of mask can easily be made by using traditional papier maché, but will probably take longer to make and to dry.

106 *Space Bride.* The headdress is based on a hat with a scarf attached, the rolled paper tubes are secured on a light framework of chicken wire, and when in position the framework covered with paper strips soaked in Polycell or similar paste. When dry, table tennis balls were added, and the scarf and hat brim painted with Helizarin Binder D and silver powder to keep the fabric soft for draping, the rest was sprayed with a silver paint spray. Silver painted sunglasses were added to complete the effect. The remainder of the costume was made from old nylon curtains and painted nylon net

CONSTRUCTIONS AND ARMATURES

The 'skeleton' method based on the style of a fencing mask in chicken wire or wire ribs may be found useful, as may strips of card or stiff paper made into a frame work. Wire may be wrapped with strips of rag to help to secure sharp joints, or to provide a surface which can be sewn. The method of casting on a balloon in several layers of paper and glue (the balloon is subsequently burst) is useful and diverting for children.

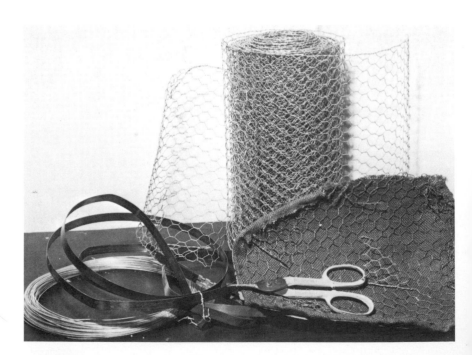

107 Useful and necessary materials for making masks with wire frames, showing underside of simple wire frame mask covered with hessian

108 Mask/helmet made from chicken wire, coarsely woven with a great variety of torn fabric, with added buckles, beads etc. Tassels are made from dyed unspun wool (factory waste)

109 Mask based on wire frame, in the course of construction. This is to be a cow, the horns are made from Mod-Roc-covered wire, the eyes are paper covered table tennis balls and the entire frame is covered with pasted paper

110 Mask-type helmet, covering most of the face, made from chicken wire layered with newspaper soaked in Marvin-medium. The crest is polystyrene bound to a cardboard form with tissue paper and paste, painted with various gold powders (no spray as this dissolves the polystyrene)

111 Helmet mask in chicken wire, a method not really suitable for young children. The mask is half-layered in pasted newspaper painted black. The visor is card with a red painted device

112 Viking-type helmet mask, partly
covering the face; the wire structure is
covered with 'American Cloth' painted
dark bronze and decorated with studs
outlined with string. The horns are wire
bound with string

113 Very large mask (three-feet high) on
wire frame covered with layers of paper
and paste. Fur and paint added

114 Egyptian-type mask; wire structure, paper covered, fabric and card decoration. Painted in blue and gold.

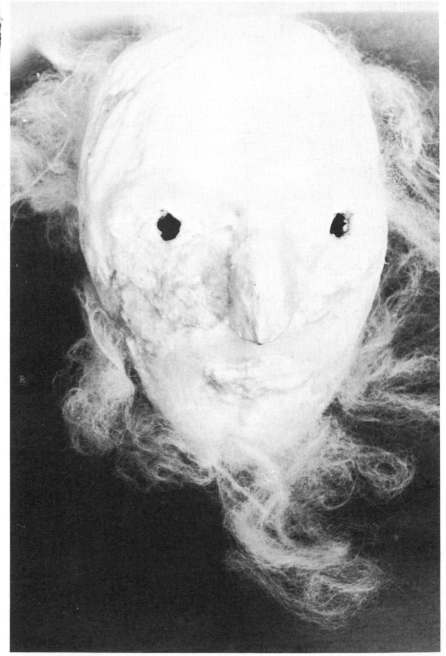

115 Wire frame mask, covered with paper strips, painted silver, unspun wool for hair and beard

116 *Winter*; based on a wire framework
covered with papier maché, decorated
with powder, paint and dried grass

117 *Chinese*; this replica is of small metal
rectangles wired onto a fabric lined
chicken-wire base through small drilled
holes. This took a long time to make, and
is not for young children to attempt since
the wire was difficult to manipulate

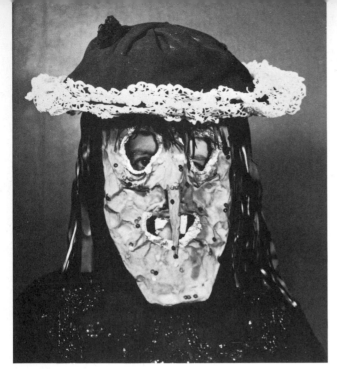

118 Brilliant-green witch, papier maché
over wire structure, with silver paper and
green sequins added. Hair made from
black PVC strips, black fabric hat with
paper doily edging. Worn with a black
Victorian beaded cape

119 Atahualpa masks. Wire structure
covered with layers of newspaper, painted
in gold and bright colours. Headdress of
yellow crepe-paper decorated with metallic
paper, fringe, star sequins and rolled
paper tubes

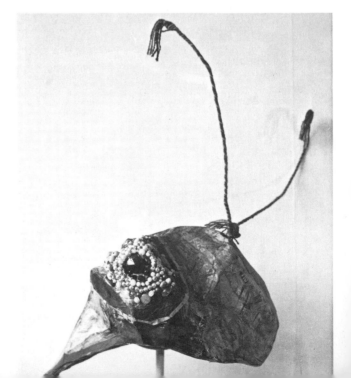

120 Wire half-mask insect, with wrapped
wire gilded antenae; enormous eyes of
many coloured beads

121 Insect helmet. Wire structure covered with green fabric, eyes made from checked cloth to suggest compound eyes

122 Large bird mask; basic structure of strong chicken wire. This required more manipulation than a young child could manage and is more suitable for senior work. The wire cage was covered with several layers of glued newspaper and the 'feathers' and beak are made of cut felt in bright yellow and black; the collar is decorated in strips of yellow-dyed hessian. Masks this size can constitute half or even whole costumes

123 Wire structure covered in papier mâché, richly painted in white, red and green, with rag hair and beard

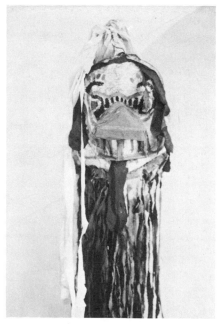

124 and 125 Mask in course of construction. This is made from strips of strong card, glued and stapled and then covered with gold-painted felt

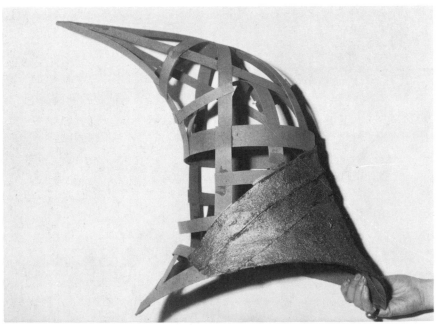

126 The final result, a South American style ritual bird mask, covered in gilded felt and decorated with pheasant feathers and feathers from feather dusters. The beak is covered with string and silver wire, the crest is part of the wire centre of a dart board with dripped Marvin-medium and dye. This mask is normally worn with a feather-trimmed cloak decorated with gold collage

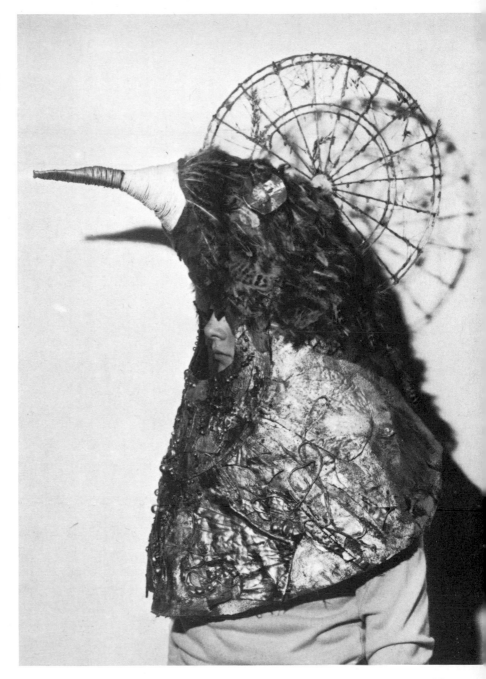

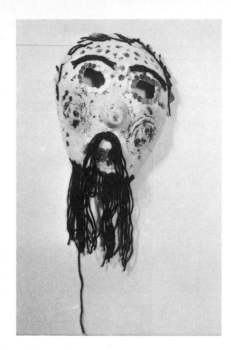

127   Mask in papier-maché, covering a
balloon which was subsequently burst,
trimmed with wool, sequins and paint. A
very simple example of a useful method of
mask making which has many possibilities

128   A balloon mask with a paper surface
applied in layers; card nose, paper and
fabric decoration, foil hair and crochet
'yashmak'. Painted gold, silver black and
green

SOFT MATERIALS

Fabrics of any kind may be used, either as surfaces for masks with a solid construction or as the main structure of the mask, as in hoods, with or without faces.

129 Most fabric scraps, old hats, braid etc will be useful for covering, decorating or making masks

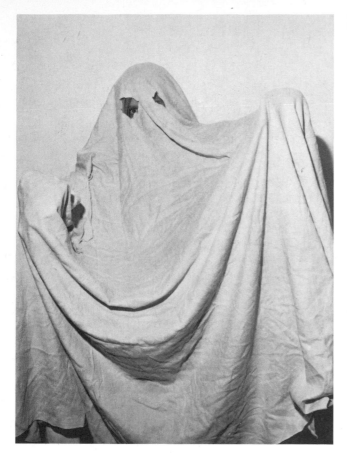

130 The usual ghost. This simple
construction, two holes in an old sheet,
may be extended and decorated to make
something as rich as one wishes using any
of the methods described in this book.

131 A simple but effective helmet mask,
made from an old hat with a brim. The
brim is cut from the back and added to the
front to extend over the face, large eyes
with black plastic eye lashes trimmed with
sequins, the rest painted silver

132 Calico shapes cut out double (no gusset needed) and glued; painted with powder paint to make a striped cat

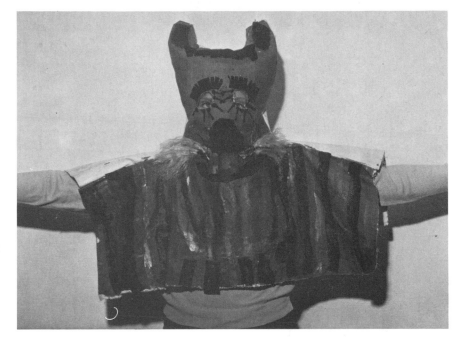

133 to 135 Showing gradual development of hood and cowl, simply cut from felt, with a minimum number of seams, gold paint and string collage, dripped with Marvin-medium or similar glue. Such masks are capable of infinite extensions and may become whole costumes

136 Felt hood. Beads extend over forehead; feathers, eye and crest are also in felt, trimmed with metallic fabric and beads. The colours are blue, red, gold and silver. This hood principle is capable of many interpretations

137 Half mask, one of a series of bird masks made for students who acted the story of *Jorida and Joringle* by Grimm. This is a card structure covered with felt and with paper 'feathers'. Stories of this sort may suggest many items of mask and costume construction

138 Bird mask in card covered in net. The 'feathers' are in fabric and paper sculpture, in green, gold, black and silver. This mask fastens round the head with an elastic band which is concealed by the 'feathers'

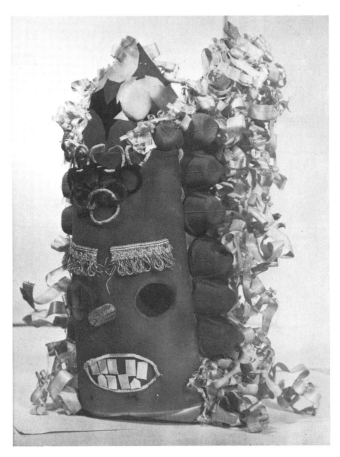

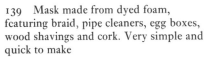

139 Mask made from dyed foam,
featuring braid, pipe cleaners, egg boxes,
wood shavings and cork. Very simple and
quick to make

140 Half mask in felt, based on the
crown of a hat with feathers, earrings and
silver foil trimming. This is a comic bird
character

141 Card cylinder covered with batik,
the snood is of folded scrim. The crown is
made from gold painted felt strips,
trimmed with packaging from a chocolate
box and small gilt baubles, the ringlets
made from swarf (metal turnings)

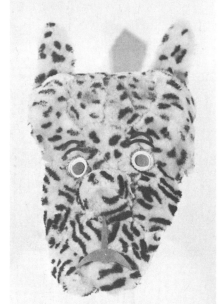

142 Wire structure covered with layered paper strips and cellular paste, and finally covered with sheepskin pieces

143 Fur fabric covered wire frame, eyes made from bottle tops with red felt centres

144 Card shape covered with fur; the nose is part of an egg box covered in shiny black plastic, the whiskers are match stalks, the tongue is felt. The eyes are made from plastic balls with painted centres

MOD-ROC AND PLASTER

'Mod-Roc' is a preparatory material similar to that used in hospitals for making plaster splints; the material is quick, easy and pleasant to use, and is very quick drying. It is capable of three-dimensional sculptural effects. This type of material may be simulated by using bandage, scrim or rag in plaster of paris, a traditional sculptors technique, and applied either to a flat surface or to a constructed armature or grid.

145 One-eyed monster made from simple wire frame covered with Mod-Roc. The horns are Mod-Roc-covered wire and are flexible and swing when the mask is worn; the hair is green raffia

146　Wire structure in the shape of a
fencing mask, with the features built from
Mod-Roc. The eyes are table tennis balls
surrounded by silver string, the hair and
beard are unwound rope dyed green, the
tongue is red fur fabric, and the moustache
is auburn hair (donated by the maker).
This mask is quite large and heavy and is
held in place by a helmet covering the
whole head

147　Simple wire frame with a thin layer
of Mod-Roc, one side of the face covered
with 'scales' made of Honesty leaves and
seeds painted silver; the eyes are built-up
from plaster and surrounded by black
string, the eye lashes are made from strips
of card

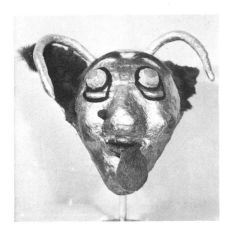

148 Mod-Roc sculpted over a balloon; the tongue and ears are fur

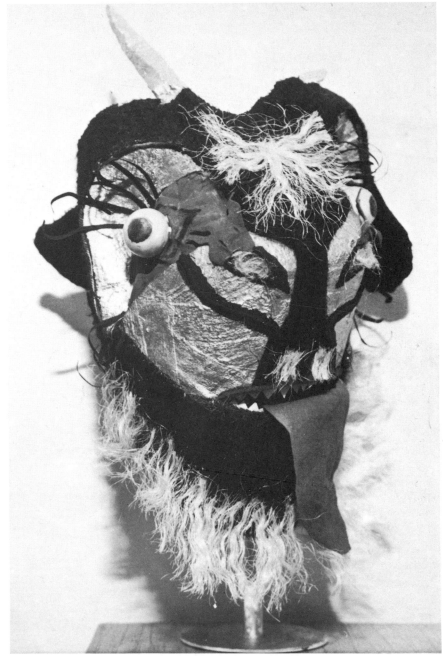

149 The shape was constructed from thin card stapled together, covered by a thin layer of Mod-Roc and then coated in parts with 'poodle-wool' fabric. The beard and fringe are of combed string, the eyes are table tennis balls, the tongue red felt

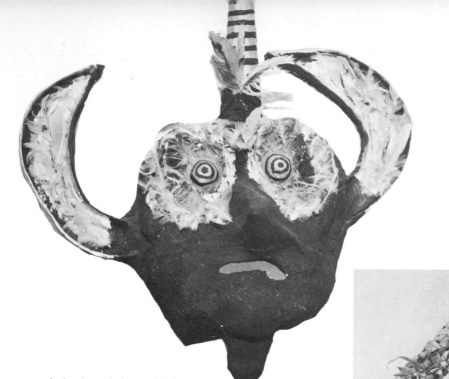

150 A simple card shape with features.
Ears or horns built up from Mod-Roc, the
eyes surrounded by feathers from a feather
duster

151 Simple card shape covered in thin
layer of Mod-Roc and then painted. The
hair is made from plaited card strips, the
teeth are melon seeds, the wart on the chin
is from frayed string

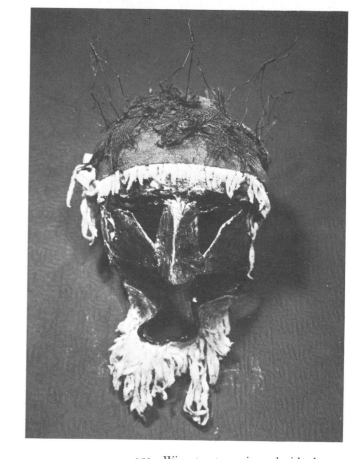

152 Wire structure trimmed with plaster, painted silver and then rubbed over with black boot polish to produce a tarnished effect; wire skeleton crown, fabric hair and beard. This could be a 'King Lear' mask

153 Wire structure skimmed with plaster, based roughly on the Sutton Hoo mask

HALF MASKS AND MASKS ON STICKS

In this section we give a range of simple and effective eye and face masks that may be used alone, or in combinations with hooded faces, or perhaps with painted faces. A series of masks can be very interesting dramatically. The back of the head may be used with one mask (the face can be painted and the mask on a stick may be reversible) or the head can be extended by means of a 'totem pole' hat. Readers will be able to think of many other refinements. Beautifully made, and this is very easy, an eye mask may become a piece of jewellery.

154 Simple mask and headdress made from cut cartridge paper. The 'hair' is curled with the edge of a knife and glued onto a simple paper base

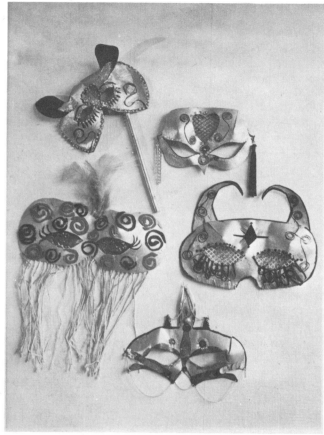

155 and 156 Half-masks on sticks. Sugar paper shapes with cut darts to form shapes, trimmed with string, threads, felt shapes, beads, tassells etc. Some are velvet covered

157 Simple half-mask made from sunglasses frame covered with small fabric flowers, (coarse lace edging will do just as well) worn with a hat made from a swimming cap covered with artificial flowers sprayed gold

158　A very simple flat mask on a stick,
quickly made with bead decoration

159　Mask on stick, flat sugar paper shape,
no darts, richly painted; some real
feathers some painted feathers, string
trimming. Eye grills from a string vest

160 A very simple card mask mounted on a stick (wooden dowelling). Teeth and nose cut from card, eye lashes from half an egg box, hair from raffia. Other details painted on in yellow, red and white. Easily made by young children, effective out of all proportion to the expertise needed

161 Simple flat mask with twig and fringe decoration

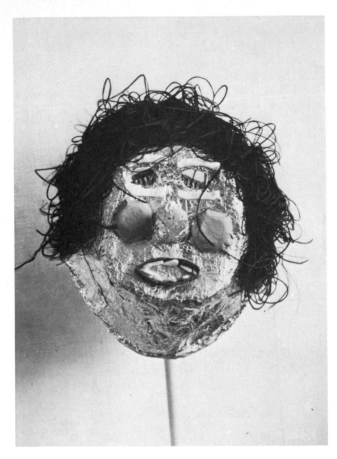

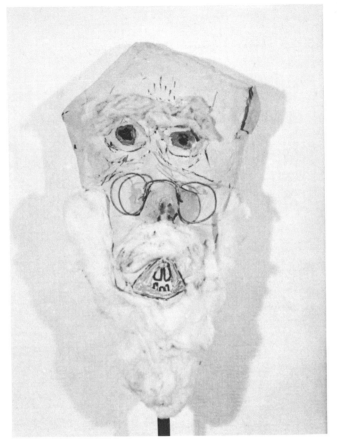

162 Sugar-paper shape covered in foil.
Polystyrene chip teeth, nose and cheeks
from egg cartons, hair from industrial
nylon waste.

163 Wire frame, paper layers, wire
spectacles, cotton wool whiskers,
cardboard teeth

164 and 165 Powder-paint containers have been cut with tin snips to make this half-mask; the shapes are held together with soft wire through holes made with a hammer and a nail, the effect is Siamese. The felt lining covers all the wire ends, preventing the mask from scratching the face.

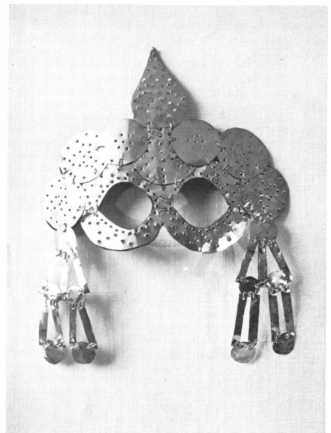

166 Small mask, more in the nature of a
rod puppett. The scissors are inserted
between layers of squashed tin can, parts
of other cans are added together with many
small metal objects. Marvin-medium was
used to glue the parts together

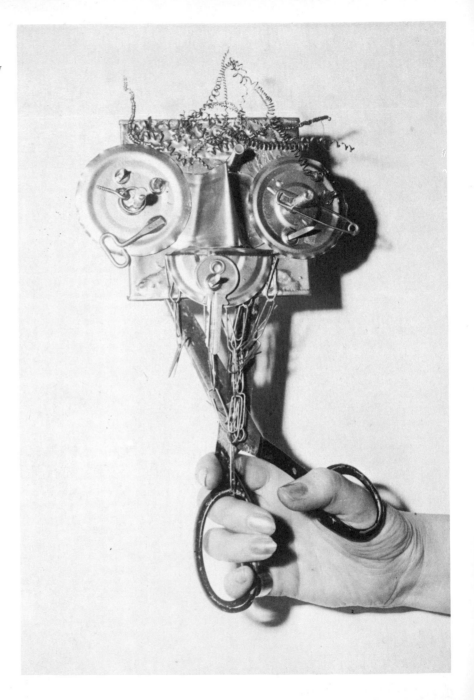

WEAVING, KNITTING AND SIMILAR CRAFTS

The textile crafts are becoming more and more popular and many people are becoming experts. Too often, tatting, crochet and knitting are used purely as craft to make lamps or belts, or they are used in a pleasant but rather stylised way to make the standard wall hanging. A more adventurous and creative use, experimenting a little, and not being too rule-bound will be found very useful in mask-making. Such techniques can be used in any of the ways discussed in the chapter on soft materials. Do not ignore paper weaving, the person who enjoys this kind of planning can produce some splendid effects.

167　Some suggested materials

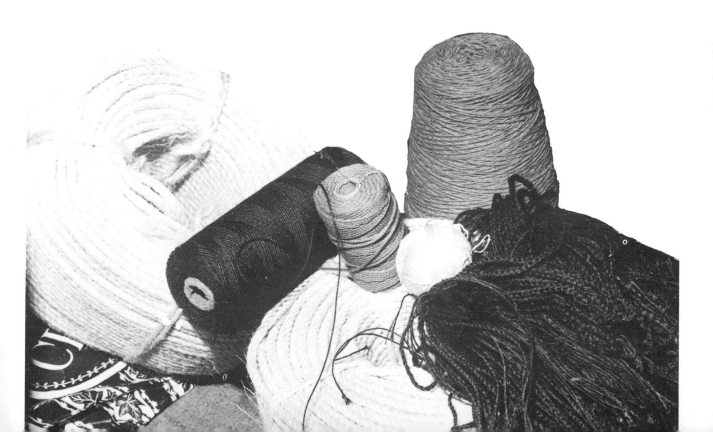

168 to 170   Macramé mask; very intricate (not for beginners) using many knots and three thicknesses of twine and incorporating wooden beads. This mask forms a complete headdress and laces down the back. With time and patience, this could be a full costume or a piece of soft sculpture.

171   Soft mask, plain knitted in tweed
wool. Eyes and mouth openings sewn with
button-hole or blanket stitch, suede
patches and small shells added. The head
covering is patchwork suede

172 and 173   Knitted mask made in
pieces and sewn together to form a hood.
Simple and effective, made by an
eight-year old girl who was inspired by
the mask shown in 171.

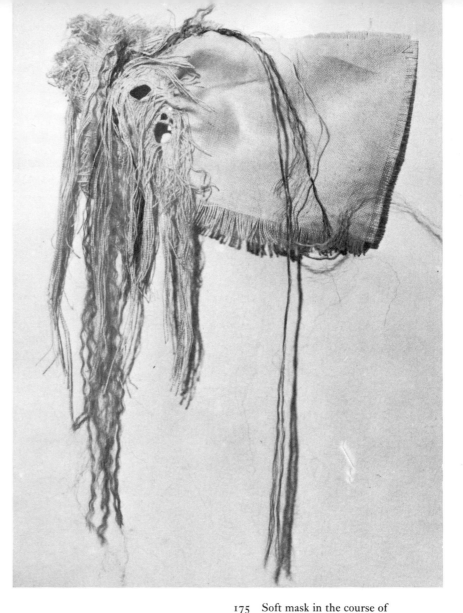

174 Large mask, cane structure with thick string warp, detail woven in felt strips, braid etc. This kind of mask may extend from head to toe

175 Soft mask in the course of construction from hessian, pulled and drawn threads, ruching and over-stitching using the pulled out threads. Other waste materials to make long hair

176 Woven paper mask in black and white. This method required careful handling. The warp readily serves as hair and beard when the weft is omitted. A time-consuming method but capable of a great variety of interpretations

INTERESTING SURFACES

It will be seen from our examples that the most ordinary mask made by any of several methods already described, may be enlivened by the use of surface patterns. This can be a lengthy process, but the results can be quite beautiful. If this kind of work is being set by a teacher, it may be an idea to give a theme, which may be carried out in a wide range of surface materials; there are vast possibilities for creative thinking.

177 A few ideas for making interesting surfaces.

178 and 179 Mask headdress with a
Siamese effect; it is a card structure
covered with rice and peas with curls of
paper and metal waste, the whole sprayed
silver

180 A very simple card mask with extensions in paper and egg boxes. A cylinder of card has been deeply cut away at the sides, producing the effect of a beard on which bottle tops (hammered flat) have been mounted; note the careful production of a regular scale pattern. We feel that this is a successful way of using foil shapes

181 Card construction beneath silver foil and Christmas tree foil strips. The crown is of card shapes covered with foil. A still photograph cannot do justice to this kind of mask, as it needs to be seen in motion. This mask is called *Frost* and it tinkles and rustles as it moves. The principle of using sounds in masks by adding percussion items such as rattles, bells etc, should be noted

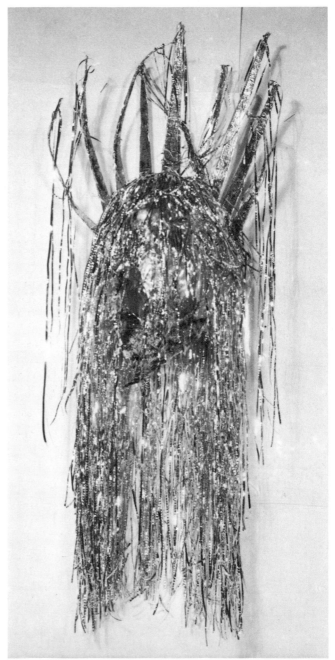

182 Apple boxes, rice on card, cardboard tubes cut into slices for headdress decoration, nylon veil and metallic party ribbon, all painted gold. The basic cylinder is net-covered card

183 A half-mask consisting of a hood entirely covered with small blue feathers and with a card beak

184   Bird mask in wire, covered with pleated scarlet fabric, with black satin eyes with gold sequins, trimmed with gold painted artificial flowers, beads and sequins. The beak and wattles are carefully covered with shiny chocolate papers in bright colours. Large size wood shavings sprayed gold and bronze have been applied individually. Please note that the application of shavings etc requires great patience

185 Simple card shape with dead-match patterned surface. The collection of matches can be laborious but often people are willing to help and in our opinion the results justify the time spent. The mask was originally mounted on a shield to simulate the eclipse of the Sun when the legend of Phaeton was being dramatised

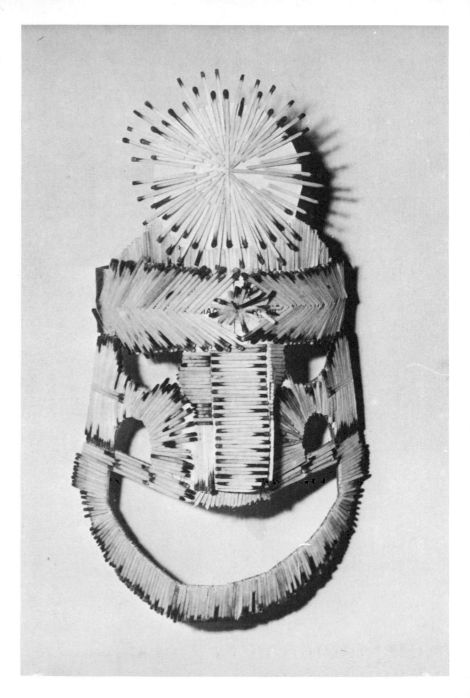

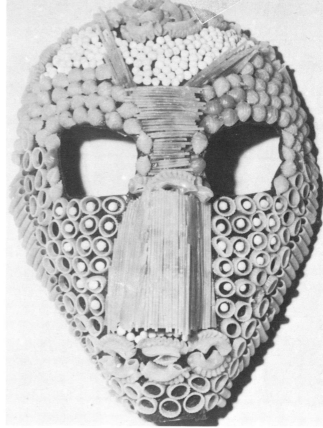

186   Bird mask on wire structure, with
card beak painted orange, entirely covered
with dark wood shavings. Some of these
shavings were glued one at a time; the
very small ones were crushed and sprinkled
onto thick paste or glue

187   Mask cast on a balloon by means of
cellular paste and paper strips. Various
kinds of pasta have been used for the
surface. Pasta and dried seeds of all kinds
are useful for this purpose and are in a way
reminiscent of Aztec mosaic surfaces

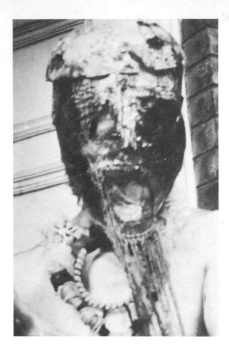

188 *The Beekeeper*. Based on a wire frame layered with paper and painted gold, the helmet and crown are made from parts of an old pan and colander found on the beach. The beard is rayon fringe, the eye sockets are covered with black net, and many small objects have been added. The reference is partly to the character of Beowulf, and an approximately Anglo-Saxon effect was intended. The 'skull' is covered with sheepskin

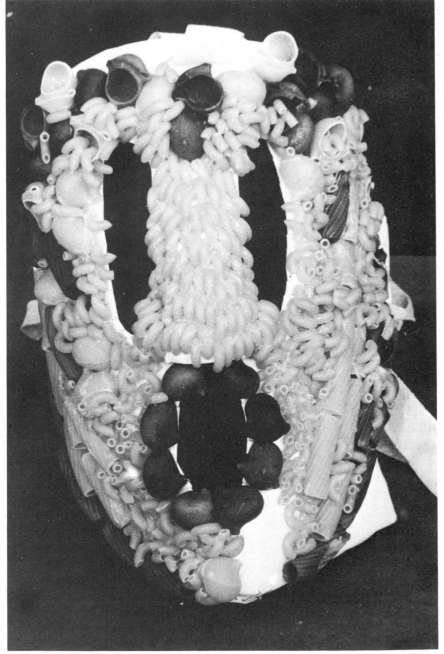

189 Paper shape covered in various kinds of pasta

FURTHER READING

The following books will be found inspirational and, in many cases, directly useful in mask making activities.

Masks and How to Make Them, Slade, Faber & Faber.
Making Masks, Barbara Snook, Batsford.
Paper Faces, M. Grater, Mills and Boon.
Children Make Sculpture, Elizabeth Leyh, Van Nostrand Reinhold.
Art and Ideas for Young People, Pearl Greenberg, Van Nostrand Reinhold.
Introducing Macramé, Eirian Short, Batsford.
Pre-Columbian Art, Hans van Winning, Thames & Hudson.
Primitive Art, Frazer, Thames & Hudson.
African Art, Frank Willett, Thames & Hudson.
Eskimo Masks, Ray, University of Washington Press.
African & Oceanic Art, Lowell & Neverman, Abrams.
Mexican and Central American Art, I. Nicholson, Hamlyn.
The Technique of Woven Tapestry, Tadek Beutlich, Batsford.
Designing with String, Mary Seyd, Batsford.
Paper Sculpture, George Borchard, Batsford.
Making Paper Costumes, Janet Boyes, Batsford.
Model Making in Schools, Brenda B. Jackson, Batsford.